The Foolish, Timid Rabbit

Written by Lou Kuenzler

Illustrated by Beatrice Bencivenni

Collins

There was a crash. Thumper shook with fear.

He ran to tell Buck.

"Did you hear that crash?" said Thumper. "I think the planet will crack!"

4

5

They ran by Vixen.

The planet will split.

We must tell the king.

The pals sped by Tusker.

The planet will snap apart.

8

"Stop!" said the king.
"What is the matter?"

"Did you hear that crash?"
Thumper said.

The king said, "Look. It was just a nut!"

11

Then Thumper went red.

"We can stop," he said. "The planet will not crack!"

Will the planet crack?

Review: After reading

Use your assessment from hearing the children read to choose any GPCs, words or tricky words that need additional practice.

Read 1: Decoding

- Practise reading words that contain adjacent consonants. Model sounding out the following word, saying each of the sounds quickly and clearly. Then blend the sounds together.
  c/r/a/sh   crash
- Ask the children to find another word that starts with the two letters **c** and **r** on page 4. (*crack*)
- Look at page 6 together. Ask the children to sound out the words **planet** and **split**.

Read 2: Prosody

- Model reading each page with expression to the children.
- After you have read each page, ask the children to have a go at reading with expression.
- Have fun reading the book together, with you reading the main text and the children reading the speech bubbles.

Read 3: Comprehension

- For every question ask the children how they know the answer. Ask:
  o What happened to Thumper at the start of the story?
  o Why did Thumper go red when the King told them it was just a nut?
  o What would you have said to Thumper when he went red?
  o What do you think Thumper would do if he heard another crash?